EXPLORING AI

by Gaelen Hadlett

CAPSTONE PRESS
a capstone imprint

Published by Spotlight, an imprint of Capstone
1710 Roe Crest Drive, North Mankato, Minnesota 56003
capstonepub.com

Library of Congress Cataloging-in-Publication Data is available on the Library of Congress website.

ISBN: 9781669074649 (hardcover)
ISBN: 9781669074656 (paperback)
ISBN: 9781669074663 (ebook pdf)

Summary: Explore the world of artificial intelligence and the amazing impact it is having on daily life. Discover how people are using artificial intelligence to try to solve issues with health, the environment, endangered animals, and more! In collaboration with the International Society for Technology in Education (ISTE), this book features an engaging narrative and dynamic photos that explore the creators of today's AI and those who will be taking it into the future—like you!

Editorial Credits
Editor: Erika L. Shores; Designer: Hilary Wacholz; Media Researcher: Jo Miller; Production Specialist: Tori Abraham

Image Credits
Alamy: Stocktrek Images, Inc., 21; Associated Press: Christophe Ena, 18; Getty Images: FG Trade, 11, Ignatiev, 16, ipopba, Cover (top), John Fedele, 7, Jordi Salas, 23, metamorworks, 29, Paul Souders, 20, Shutter2U, Cover (bottom); Science Source: USGS, 19; Shutterstock: Adrian Parker, 24, Andrey Suslov, Cover (middle, background), Chansom Pantip, 9, Gluiki, design element (throughout), Gorodenkoff, 10, 14, Ground Picture, 28, ImageFlow, 5, Microgen, 22, Mila Supinskaya Glashchenko, 25, Ole.CNX, 4, Potapov Alexander, 17, Pressmaster, 6, 27, sfam_photo, 15, ShadeDesign, 13

This book is published in partnership with the International Society for Technology in Education (ISTE).

All internet sites appearing in back matter were available and accurate when this book was sent to press.

Printed and bound in China. 5593

TABLE OF CONTENTS

INTRODUCTION
All About AI 4

CHAPTER 1
AI Helps People 8

CHAPTER 2
AI and the Environment 18

CHAPTER 3
AI Uncovers the Past 22

CHAPTER 4
The Humans Behind AI 26

Glossary 30

Read More 31

Internet Sites 31

Index 32

About the Author 32

Words in **BOLD** are in the glossary.

All About AI

Recognizing faces of wild animals. Detecting early signs of cancer. Identifying ancient artifacts. Artificial intelligence (AI) can do amazing things.

AI is the ability of a computer to "think" like a human. Computers with AI can solve problems on their own. New discoveries are being made every day by people working to develop AI. AI doesn't just exist in a computer lab, though. You have probably interacted with **virtual assistants**, **chatbots**, and other AI on phones and video games. What are some of the other ways AI helps people? How did this AI develop, and who are the humans responsible for making it?

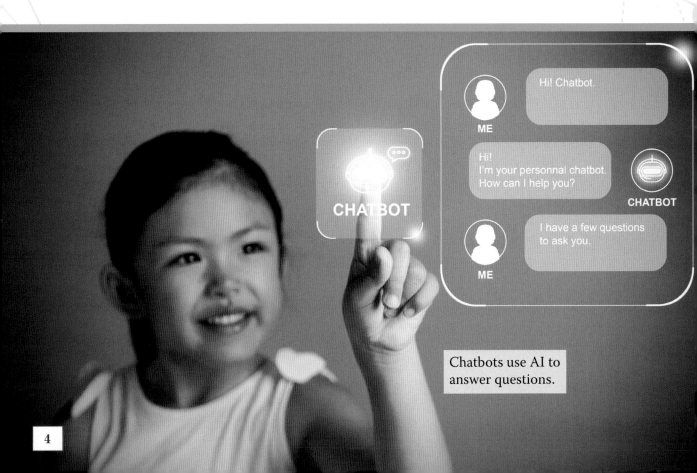

Chatbots use AI to answer questions.

AI tools can recognize faces to unlock cellphones.

Thinking Machines

Artificial intelligence isn't a new idea. Long before computers were invented, both the ancient Greeks and Chinese created automata. These kinds of machines have moving parts that operate on their own, like a cuckoo clock. People at the time wondered if these machines could think.

In 1950, computer scientist Alan Turing came up with a test to help decide if a computer was intelligent. His test was simple. An interviewer, a person, and a computer program—each in a different room—would all chat through text on a screen. If the interviewer could not tell which of the two other participants was a computer, then the computer passed. Passing the test meant the computer was "thinking" like a human. No computers could pass Turing's test.

Dreaming of AI

Scientists long dreamed about the creation of AI. An early success was ELIZA, a chatbot created by Joseph Weizenbaum at Massachusetts Institute of Technology (MIT) from 1964 to 1966. ELIZA was designed to act like a therapist. It would respond to every statement made by a human user by asking a question about the human's previous statement. At the time, many people were impressed with this early AI.

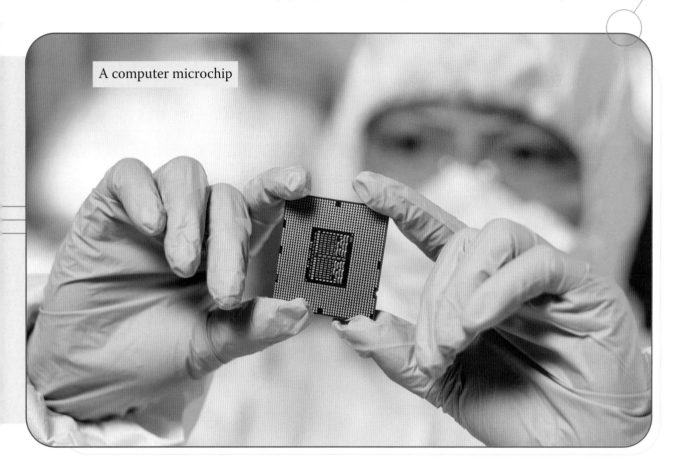

A computer microchip

Scientists hoped for more AI advancements in the 1970s and 1980s. But computer hardware wasn't yet up to the task. Computer processors—microchips that run the instructions of computer programs—were not fast enough. The mathematical formulas were not advanced enough either.

While **computer engineers** built faster and more advanced computer hardware, researchers and designers worked on developing new computer programs. By working together and not giving up, they brought about the AI we have today. It can find tumors, listen to whales, measure pollution, and so much more!

People worked together to develop the hardware and software needed for AI.

CHAPTER 1

AI Helps People

Artificial intelligence is a tool. AI can **analyze** certain situations much faster than humans. Let's take a close look at AI tools developed to help people in two important ways.

AI Describes What's on the Screen

AI can help people who are **visually impaired** know what is being shown on a screen. Ideally, all digital pictures or videos would include a text description that could be read out loud by a computer. Unfortunately, a lot of digital media available today does not include descriptions. AI is changing that.

AI designers create tools that **generate** a text description of a photo or clip of video. The text can then be used by a computer program called a screen reader to read the text out loud. Instead of needing a human to describe digital images, the AI can describe the content.

An AI tool that describes images on a screen can be used by people with visual impairment.

Developing this AI tool was not easy. How it works is that the AI uses machine learning **algorithms** that analyze large sets of **data**. Data can be articles, images, videos, and chat conversations. By analyzing all this data, AI tries to "learn" how to perform a specific task, such as describing what's in a photo on a screen.

A data center is the place where data is collected and stored.

What Is a Machine Learning Algorithm?

An algorithm is a repeatable set of steps that may create an output. An algorithm has inputs, procedure, and outputs. For example, imagine an algorithm for braiding hair. The input could be any type of hair or even a hair-like material, such as yarn or thread. The procedure is a set of steps that are applied to the hair. The output would be a complete braid using the input material.

AI algorithms for braiding might be trained on pictures of many types of braids. The quality of the training data and process are important. The AI algorithm might produce a typical braid. It could also produce interesting new braids or knotty hair styles that aren't braids at all.

Training Data Helps AI Learn

Algorithms learn from data called training data. Training datasets can be quite large. Some training data contain five billion image and text pairings! It took years for humans to collect and analyze some training datasets. Most of the data had to first be analyzed by people, not computers, before it could be used for training. People need to identify important pieces of the data and write paragraphs describing images and videos. AI would not be possible without humans first collecting and describing the data.

The data used in AI tools first needed to be described by a human.

Making a Model

Most modern AI uses machine learning algorithms. One such type of algorithm, a **neural network**, uses training data to learn. Scientists developed the idea for a neural network by studying how human brains learn and grow. Neural network gets its name from the layered and connected structure of **neurons** in our brains.

AI needs learning models in order to work. These models are created using complex math and training data that focuses on learning a specific task. A model is like a program or app that combines the algorithm, math, and information about the data for computers to use. The math is so complicated, many AI designers and engineers cannot even explain how or why a model works.

After creating a model, AI designers try it out with a smaller set of training data as well as newly collected data. If the model doesn't work, they might need to make small changes to it or start over. Sometimes a model needs more or different data to train on.

USE YOUR BRAIN!

Imagine an AI tool for grading homework. Your teacher gives your homework to the AI tool, and it provides feedback and a grade. Your teacher no longer spends time grading assignments. The AI saves your teacher a lot of time. What would be the pros and cons of receiving only AI feedback and nothing from your teacher?

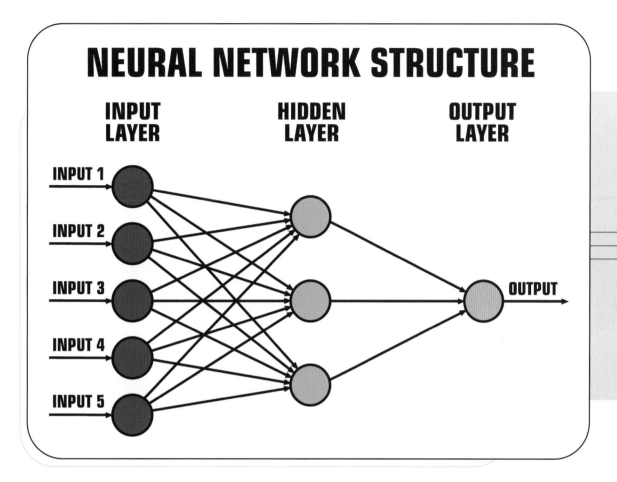

NEURAL NETWORK STRUCTURE

INPUT LAYER — **HIDDEN LAYER** — **OUTPUT LAYER**

INPUT 1
INPUT 2
INPUT 3
INPUT 4
INPUT 5

OUTPUT

Improving Your AI Recipe with Parameters

After creating a model using a dataset to train an AI algorithm, the designer works within parameters to tweak how the model runs. Think of parameters like the amount of an ingredient you use in a recipe. Instead of using sugar and flour like you would to bake cookies, with AI models, you would use data.

AI parameters are called weights. The weights determine how much emphasis the AI should give to different parts of its model. A low weight value gives that part less meaning. A high weight value gives that part more meaning. Different weights can make a big difference in the AI, just like using a cup of sugar instead of a teaspoon would make a big difference in the sweetness of your cookies!

Parameters help guide the AI. The AI designer needs to try out different weights to see which values give the best or most accurate responses from the AI.

AI Finds Cancer

AI can help doctors detect diseases such as cancer. Detecting cancer early improves treatment and helps save lives.

Doctors often take images, such as X-rays or CT scans, to look for cancer in the body. These scans are taken digitally—and digital images are perfect for analysis by AI. AI researchers build training datasets based on images collected by doctors and patients. In this case, doctors help build the training data by identifying whether cancer appears in the images.

For an AI tool focused on early detection of brain cancer, the training data might contain thousands of images of brains. Each image is paired with data from a doctor to determine if cancer is present and where it is located. The AI designer uses this data to train a machine learning model.

A doctor analyzes digital scans so their examination can be stored as data.

The model neural network is made up of a series of layers. Each layer focuses on a piece of data and passes the data along to the next layer. For example, the first layer might focus on what the edges of a tumor could look like. The next layer looks at what the shape of a tumor might look like. Another layer focuses on different textures of a tumor.

An AI tool helps pinpoint potential cancer so a doctor can verify it and prescribe treatment.

What happens as an image passes through the layers of the neural network? The AI tool might first detect 15 different potential edges of a tumor. It passes those locations to the next layer, which combines those edges into one potential shape of a tumor. It passes that shape to the next layer, which may or may not identify the texture of the shape as a tumor.

A doctor needs to look at a whole image of a brain to try to spot tumors. But an AI tool can look at an image **pixel** by pixel. Doctors use it to find much smaller and harder-to-notice areas that could lead to cancer.

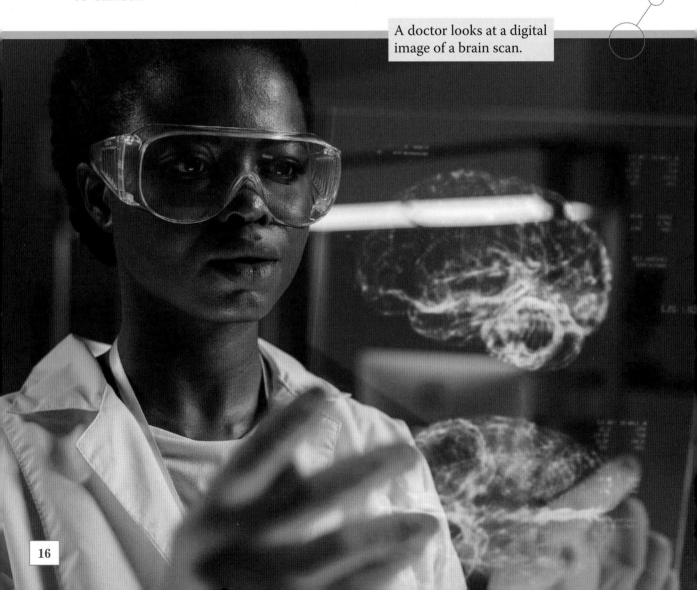

A doctor looks at a digital image of a brain scan.

Although it's called machine learning, the learning done by AI algorithms is really using a combination of complex mathematical formulas to make calculated guesses. The AI's guesses aren't always right. A doctor must double check and confirm the AI's output.

AI Can Get It Wrong

It is important to point out that AI's answers are not always accurate. So AI designers create tests to measure the quality of their AI. Their tests may ask the AI to answer a true or false question.

For example, an AI that can describe photos might be asked, "Is this a picture of a duck?" The AI might answer "no" if the type of duck was not part of its dataset. This is an example of a false negative. A false negative is when an AI answers "no" or "false" when the answer is actually "yes" or "true."

A false positive is the opposite. The AI is shown a picture of a swan and asked again, "Is this a picture of a duck?" The AI answers "yes." This would happen if the dataset had incorrectly labeled pictures of swans as if they were ducks. A false positive is when AI answers "yes" or "true" when the correct answer is "no" or "false."

AI designers test the false-positive rate and false-negative rate to measure the quality of their AI. No AI is correct 100 percent of the time.

CHAPTER 2

AI and the Environment

Protecting our land, water, plants, and animals is necessary to humankind. Many scientists are using artificial intelligence to tackle threats to the environment.

Satellites in Space Use AI to Analyze Lake Water

Lake Chad in central Africa has shrunk over the last 50 years. As it shrinks, the lake's water is in danger of becoming unsafe. The lake provides water to more than 40 million people in Chad, Cameroon, Niger, and Nigeria.

Lake Chad

The UNESCO World Water Quality **Portal** for Lake Chad uses **satellite** imagery along with machine learning models to analyze the lake's water. This AI can report when water quality drops to alert officials. Then officials can look at what is causing this drop and keep track of it over time.

The AI powering this project uses real-time data from satellites. The satellites record high-quality data—more than just a picture from space. They have **sensors** to collect data on water level, temperature, and other information.

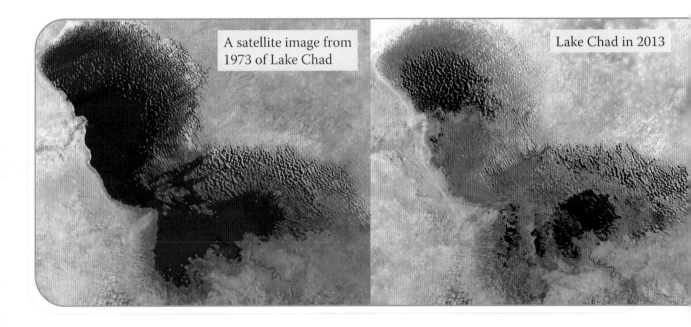

A satellite image from 1973 of Lake Chad

Lake Chad in 2013

Researchers created training data combining the satellite imagery, water quality samples, and other climate data. The training data was analyzed by a machine learning algorithm. It determined how colors and other sensor data from the satellites related to the water quality tests. The satellites and the machine learning algorithm can pick up much smaller changes in color than the human eye. This data combined with the algorithm created an AI model that quickly determined water quality of the lake.

Beluga Whales and AI

Beluga whales have been endangered since 2008. Scientists know underwater noise pollution, along with climate change, affects the whales' habitat and population. Scientists at the National Oceanic and Atmospheric Administration (NOAA) are using AI to help keep track of them and monitor their behavior.

Over time, the whales' habitat near Alaska has become a busy shipping and fishing route, which creates a lot of underwater noise. NOAA scientists place underwater microphones in the beluga whales' habitat to analyze the noise. Scientists have been digitally recording underwater sounds in this way for years. Analyzing the sound recordings is difficult and takes a long time. Six months of recordings can take two weeks for humans to analyze. Since the recordings are digital, analyzing the data takes just a few hours with AI.

Beluga whales use sounds to communicate with each other.

To come up with a machine learning model, data scientists needed to create a training dataset with many underwater sounds. They had to collect sounds for different kinds of boats, whales, and other sea creatures. Then a machine learning algorithm was trained to identify only beluga whale sounds. Scientists use those sounds to keep track of the whales living in the area and easily notice any changes in their numbers.

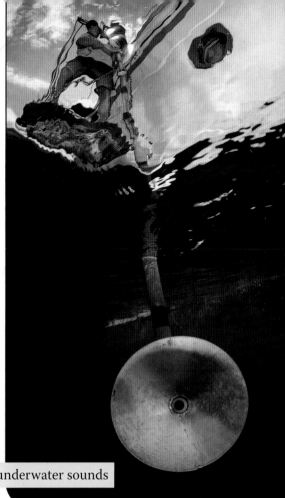

Recording underwater sounds

Whose Face Is That?

AI designers have created technology to recognize the faces of lemurs, giraffes, and other endangered animals. The algorithms work like the algorithms for human facial recognition. But instead of using human faces in the training data, they use faces of the animal species that are being studied. AI designers make models for different animal species, and the models pick up on the unique features and differences of two animals of the same species.

Typically, scientists put trackers on animals to identify each individual animal. These wearable trackers, like GPS bracelets, bother wildlife and often break. Instead, cameras can be set up around animals' habitats. This way, scientists can track the endangered species using animal-facial recognition without interfering with the animals.

CHAPTER 3

AI Uncovers the Past

Archaeologists learn about the past by studying artifacts. Artifacts are objects made by people long ago. Archaeologists along with computer scientists are using AI to preserve human history.

What's That Artifact?

Archaeologists dig up pieces of ceramic artifacts. These ancient objects are called potsherd, or sherd for short. Some are more than a thousand years old.

Without the help of AI, identifying sherds can take archeologists a long time.

Much of archaeologists' time is spent researching and identifying the sherds. They look at artifacts in books and research catalogs to find a match. Doing this research takes a lot of time. Archaeologists discovered a way for AI to help them. They worked with AI designers to develop digital tools that can recognize and categorize new sherds found around the world.

ArchAIDE, a set of apps and AI tools, uses machine learning AI. Most of the data needed for their dataset was in paper catalogs. To create the dataset, researchers made a digital copy of every photo and text printed in the catalogs. The AI model trained on the digital photos and descriptions.

Archeologists at a dig site use technology to identify and keep track of artifacts they uncover.

Machine learning engineers designed a neural network to scan the dataset of artifacts. The neural network was first trained to recognize different styles of artwork on sherds. Recognizing artwork can help identify what **culture** created the pottery and what time period it may have been created.

AI designers also trained a second neural network to recognize the shape of the sherd. Although a sherd is only a small part of a larger piece of pottery, scientists can still identify whether it came from a bowl, jar, or other object. The AI learned to identify a sherd as a piece of a bowl, jar, or other object based off a dataset and 3D models of unbroken pottery.

Artwork on sherds helped train data used by the AI tool.

An archeologist uses an app to identify an artifact.

Engineers created an app for archaeologists to use the new AI tools. When an archaeologist discovers a sherd, they take a picture of it. The app analyzes the photo and compares it to all the other sherds in the complete dataset. If the app finds a similar piece, it will tell the archaeologist and match the sherd to a type of pottery. The app also adds each new image to the dataset so the AI can keep learning. This saves archaeologists a lot of time. They can keep digging and finding more artifacts from the past.

The Humans Behind AI

AI may involve computers "thinking" for themselves, but it requires people to develop it. Remember the earlier example about an AI tool for grading homework? Who are the people needed to create the AI? Think about all the different jobs involved in creating this AI tool. Which job would you want to do?

Who Gathers the Data?

The algorithms powering AI are created by researchers and designers. For an AI that grades homework, they would ask teachers questions to find out what they would want a grading tool to do.

Next, researchers and designers would work with data scientists. The dataset needed for the AI algorithm to learn from could have billions of images, math problems, grading guides, diagrams, and texts. Data scientists figure out ways to organize and analyze the data.

Data scientists work with data taggers, or data labelers. They provide the human knowledge that many AI algorithms need to learn from in a dataset. They write descriptions of an image, diagram, or other piece of data.

Who Puts It to Work?

Machine learning engineers turn AI algorithms into applications. These engineers create the app a teacher would use to grade homework.

Computer engineers develop the processors and microchips to make AI run faster. Regular processors are designed to run typical applications. Computer engineers design processors that are made for training and running AI models.

Computer engineers inspect computer hardware.

USE YOUR BRAIN!

Use your brain to program a pretend robot! Ask an adult to be your "robot." Write down step-by-step instructions for your robot to follow to hand out a snack for the class.

After attempting the task, ask what data an AI-powered robot might need to complete the task.

Responsible AI

AI **ethics** means creating AI responsibly. The people who study and work to make sure AI is responsible are called AI ethicists. An AI ethicist would think about whether an AI that grades homework is fair and benefits all students.

AI ethicists can point out flaws in AI, like when the training data is incomplete or doesn't represent all cultures. Flaws in AI can come in many forms. It can be **biased** in how it answers questions. It can leave out groups of people, such as the very old or the very young. Without people to keep an eye on how AI is created and used, AI programs could lead to more unfairness throughout the world.

Students work together to build and program a robot.

AI and You

AI tools are helping find cancer, address pollution, and learn about people from long ago. AI may drive a car entirely on its own and even grade your homework! The possibilities of AI are endless. But AI needs people from all backgrounds to use their experiences and views to design and develop it. It takes scientists, artists, engineers, writers, and people like you!

USE YOUR BRAIN!

Artificial intelligence learns from data created by people. People sometimes write incorrect facts or mistruths. They have biases and prejudice. Does it matter if what you are reading, watching, or playing was made by an AI? Perhaps this book was written by an AI. If it was, how would you know?

How Do You Feel About AI?

1. Would you rather have media, such as pictures, videos, books, and articles created by humans or AI?

2. Would you still trust information from media generated by AI?

3. Is the information in this book more reliable if it were written by a human or an AI?

Glossary

algorithm (AL-goh-rithm)—a step-by-step method for solving a problem or accomplishing a goal

analyze (AN-uh-lize)—to examine something carefully in order to understand it

archaeologist (ar-kee-AH-luh-jist)—a scientist who learns about the past by digging up old buildings or objects and studying them

bias (BYE-uhs)—favoring one person or point of view over another

chatbot (CHAT-bot)—a computer program designed to simulate a human conversation

computer engineer (kuhm-PYOO-tuhr en-juh-NEER)—someone trained to build and design computers

culture (KUHL-chur)—a group of people's way of life, ideas, art, customs, and traditions

data (DAY-tuh)—information stored on a computer

ethics (ETH-iks)—a set of moral issues that deals with ideas about right or wrong

generate (JEN-uh-rayt)—to bring into existence

neural network (NOO-ruhl NET-wurk)—a series of algorithms that seek to identify patterns in a dataset through a process inspired by how the human brain works

neuron (NOO-rahn)—a nerve cell that is the basic working unit of the nervous system

parameter (pa-RAM-uh-tur)—a number that can change the output of a math equation

pixel (PIKS-uhl)—one of the many tiny dots on a video screen or computer monitor that make up the visual image

portal (POHR-tuhl)—a website serving as a guide or point of entry to the internet

satellite (SAT-uh-lite)—an object that orbits a planet; an artificial satellite is a spacecraft that gathers and sends information back to Earth

sensor (SEN-sor)—an instrument that measures and detects changes and sends information to a controlling device

virtual assistant (VIHR-choo-uhl uh-SIS-tuhnt)—an AI app that can answer questions that are asked or typed into it

visually impaired (VI-zhuh-uh-lee im-PAIRED)—to have experienced any amount of loss of eyesight

Read More

Kallen, Stuart A. *Exploring Hi-Tech Careers*. San Diego: ReferencePoint Press, Inc., 2022.

Simons, Lisa M. Bolt. *Super Surprising Trivia About Artificial Intelligence*. North Mankato, MN: Capstone Press, 2024.

Washburne, Sophie. *Artificial Intelligence and Smart Technology*. New York: Cavendish Square Publishing, 2023.

Internet Sites

Artificial Intelligence Facts for Kids
kids.kiddle.co/Artificial_intelligence

Careers in AI
youtu.be/NkjYjyLYvII

Crash Course: Artificial Intelligence
pbs.org/show/crash-course-artificial-intelligence

Index

AI designers, 7, 8, 12, 13, 14, 17, 21, 23, 24, 26
AI ethicists, 28
AI researchers, 7, 14, 19, 23, 26
algorithms, 10–12, 17, 19, 21, 26, 27
animals, 4, 7, 18, 20, 21
ArchAIDE, 23
artifacts, 4, 22–25
automata, 5

beluga whales, 20–21
bias, 28, 29

cancer, 4, 14–16, 28
chatbots, 4, 6
computer engineers, 7, 12, 24, 25, 27

computer hardware, 6, 7, 27
computer programs, 5, 6, 7, 8, 12
computer scientists, 5, 6, 12, 22

data scientists, 21, 26
datasets, 11–14, 17, 21, 23, 24, 25, 26
data taggers, 26

facial recognition, 4, 21
false-negative rates, 17
false-positive rates, 17

Lake Chad, 18–19
learning models, 12–15, 19, 21, 27

neural networks, 12, 15, 16, 24

parameters, 13
pollution, 7, 19, 20, 28

screen readers, 8
sound recordings, 20–21

training data, 10–12, 14, 19, 21, 23, 28
Turing, Alan, 5

virtual assistants, 4

About the Author

Gaelen Hadlett is co-founder of Sunset Spark, a nonprofit where he teaches computing and science skills to new American families. He has more than 15 years of experience as a software engineer, where he has built educational, medical, and media software and digital games used by people around the world. He has 15 years of experience teaching creative technology in public school classrooms and has taught more than 10,000 students. He loves designing robots and games with his kids. He holds a B.S. and M.S. in computer science from the University of Central Florida.